Animal Smells

Written by Sarah O'Neil

Flying Start
to Literacy®

Contents

Introduction

Some animals can make very strong smells.

These smells help the animals to stay alive.

Some animals can use strong smells
to protect themselves from other animals.

Some animals leave smells on rocks
and plants to mark their hunting grounds.

Some animals use strong smells to
attract a mate.

Using smell for protection

Some animals protect themselves by spraying a smelly liquid over animals that might attack them. This liquid stings the enemy's skin or eyes.

Skunks

Skunks can use smell for protection.

If an animal frightens a skunk, the skunk will defend itself by stamping its front feet. If this does not work, the skunk will spray a very smelly liquid onto the animal.

This stops many animals from attacking the skunk. It also means that the skunk has time to get away.

Tasmanian devils

Tasmanian devils make a strong smell when they are frightened. Other animals do not like this smell.

This smell protects the Tasmanian devils from being attacked by animals that might want to eat them.

Tasmanian devils also use their very sharp teeth and very strong bite to protect themselves.

Stink bugs

If an animal comes too close to a stink bug, the stink bug sprays out a bad-smelling liquid.

The smelly liquid stops the animal from smelling other things for some time. This makes it hard for the animal to hunt and it keeps the stink bug safe.

Turkey vultures

Very few animals attack turkey vultures.
If a turkey vulture is attacked, it
vomits the meat that it has just eaten.

The vomit smells so bad that the
attacking animals go away and
leave the turkey vulture alone.

Polecats

Polecats give off a very strong smell if they are frightened or angry.

Other animals want to get away from this smell. This helps to keep the polecat safe.

Using smell to mark territory

Some animals use smell to keep other animals out of their hunting grounds.

They mark their hunting grounds by putting a smelly liquid onto rocks and plants. This smelly liquid is not easily washed away by rain. It keeps other animals away for many months.

Hyenas

Hyenas rub themselves against the plants in their hunting grounds. This leaves a strong smell on the plants that lasts for months and keeps other hyenas away from their territory.

Foxes

Foxes mark their hunting grounds by spraying out a stink that smells a lot like a skunk's stink. This smell lasts for a long time.

Using smell to find a mate

Some animals use strong smells to attract a mate.

Goats

When it is time for a male goat to find a mate, it gives off a very strong smell. This smell helps to attract female goats.

Musk oxen

Only the strongest male musk oxen get to mate with the females.

To show that it is the strongest, a male musk ox puts a very strong smell onto the hair of its legs.

Conclusion

Being able to make strong smells is very useful for many animals.

Smells can be sprayed onto an attacking animal. Smells can be left on plants and rocks to mark an animal's hunting ground. Some animals use smells to attract a mate.

Index